Great Works Instructional Guides for Literature

¿Eres tú mi mamá?

A guide for the Spanish version of the book by P. D. Eastman
Great Works Author: Jodene Smith, M.A.

SHELL EDUCATION

Publishing Credits

Corinne Burton, M.A.Ed., *Publisher*; Conni Medina, M.A.Ed., *Editor in Chief*; Emily R. Smith, M.A.Ed., *Content Director*; Robin Erickson, *Art Director*; Lee Aucoin, *Senior Graphic Designer*; Caroline Gasca, M.S.Ed., *Senior Editor*; Stephanie Bernard, *Associate Editor*; Sam Morales, M.A., *Associate Editor*; Don Tran, *Graphic Designer*; Jill Malcolm, *Junior Graphic Designer*

Image Credits

Julie C. Wagner Shutterstock (cover); Timothy J. Bradley (interior art)

Standards

© Copyright 2010. National Governors Association Center for Best Practices and Council of Chief State School Officers. All rights reserved.

Shell Education
5301 Oceanus Drive
Huntington Beach, CA 92649-1030
www.shelleducation.com
ISBN 978-1-4258-1749-7
© 2019 Shell Educational Publishing, Inc.

The classroom teacher may reproduce copies of materials in this book for classroom use only. The reproduction of any part for an entire school or school system is strictly prohibited. No part of this publication may be transmitted, stored, or recorded in any form without written permission from the publisher.

Table of contents

How to Use This Literature Guide 4
    Theme Thoughts 4
    Vocabulary 5
    Analyzing the Literature 6
    Reader Response 6
    Guided Close Reading 6
    Making Connections 7
    Language Learning 7
    Story Elements 7
    Culminating Activity 8
    Comprehension Assessment 8
    Response to Literature 8

Correlation to the Standards 8
    Purpose and Intent of Standards 8
    How to Find Standards Correlations 8
    Standards Correlation Chart 9

About the Author—P.D. Eastman 11
    Possible Texts for Text Comparisons 11
    Cross-Curricular Connection 11

Book Summary of *Are You My Mother?* 12
    Possible Texts for Text Sets 12

Teacher Plans and Student Pages 13
    Pre-Reading Theme Thoughts 13
    Section 1: Pages 1–17 15
    Section 2: Pages 18–37 26
    Section 3: Pages 38–49 37
    Section 4: Pages 50–64 48

Post-Reading Activities 59
    Post-Reading Theme Thoughts 59
    Culminating Activity: Home, Sweet Home! 60
    Culminating Activity: Retelling the Story 62
    Comprehension Assessment 65
    Response to Literature: Looking for Mother 67

Writing Paper 70
Answer Key 71

Introduction

How to Use This Literature Guide

Today's standards demand rigor and relevance in the reading of complex texts. The units in this series guide teachers in a rich and deep exploration of worthwhile works of literature for classroom study. The most rigorous instruction can also be interesting and engaging!

Many current strategies for effective literacy instruction have been incorporated into these instructional guides for literature. Throughout the units, text-dependent questions are used to determine comprehension of the book as well as student interpretation of the vocabulary words. The books chosen for the series are complex and are exemplars of carefully crafted works of literature. Close reading is used throughout the units to guide students toward revisiting the text and using textual evidence to respond to prompts orally and in writing. Students must analyze the story elements in multiple assignments for each section of the book. All of these strategies work together to rigorously guide students through their study of literature.

The next few pages describe how to use this guide for a purposeful and meaningful literature study. Each section of this guide is set up in the same way to make it easier for you to implement the instruction in your classroom.

Theme Thoughts

The great works of literature used throughout this series have important themes that have been relevant to people for many years. Many of the themes will be discussed during the various sections of this instructional guide. However, it would also benefit students to have independent time to think about the key themes of the book.

Before students begin reading, have them complete the *Pre-Reading Theme Thoughts* (page 13). This graphic organizer will allow students to think about the themes outside the context of the story. They'll have the opportunity to evaluate statements based on important themes and defend their opinions. Be sure to keep students' papers for comparison to the *Post-Reading Theme Thoughts* (page 59). This graphic organizer is similar to the pre-reading activity. However, this time, students will be answering the questions from the point of view of one of the characters in the book. They have to think about how the character would feel about each statement and defend their thoughts. To conclude the activity, have students compare what they thought about the themes before they read the book to what the characters discovered during the story.

How to Use This Literature Guide (cont.)

Vocabulary

Each teacher reference vocabulary overview page has definitions and sentences about how key vocabulary words are used in the section. These words should be introduced and discussed with students. Students will use these words in different activities throughout the book.

On some of the vocabulary student pages, students are asked to answer text-related questions about vocabulary words from the sections. The following question stems will help you create your own vocabulary questions if you'd like to extend the discussion.

- ¿De qué manera esta palabra describe la personalidad de _____ ?
- ¿De qué manera esta palabra se relaciona con el problema del cuento?
- ¿De qué manera esta palabra te ayuda a comprender el escenario?
- Dime de qué manera esta palabra se relaciona con la idea principal del cuento.
- ¿Qué imágenes te trae a la mente esta palabra?
- ¿Por qué crees que el autor usó esta palabra?

At times, you may find that more work with the words will help students understand their meanings and importance. These quick vocabulary activities are a good way to further study the words.

- Students can play vocabulary concentration. Make one set of cards that have the words on them and another set with the definitions. Then, have students lay them out on the table and play concentration. The goal of the game is to match vocabulary words with their definitions. For early readers or language learners, the two sets of cards could be the words and pictures of the words.

- Students can create word journal entries about the words. Students choose words they think are important and then describe why they think each word is important within the book. Early readers or language learners could instead draw pictures about the words in a journal.

- Students can create puppets and use them to act out the vocabulary words from the stories. Artwork of the characters is provided on pages 62–64. Students can use these images to retell the stories using the vocabulary words. Students may also enjoy telling their own character-driven stories using vocabulary words from the original stories.

Introduction

How to Use This Literature Guide (cont.)

Analyzing the Literature

After you have read each section with students, hold a small-group or whole-class discussion. Provided on the teacher reference page for each section are leveled questions. The questions are written at two levels of complexity to allow you to decide which questions best meet the needs of your students. The Level 1 questions are typically less abstract than the Level 2 questions. These questions are focused on the various story elements, such as character, setting, and plot. Be sure to add further questions as your students discuss what they've read. For each question, a few key points are provided for your reference as you discuss the book with students.

Reader Response

In today's classrooms, there are often great readers who are below average writers. So much time and energy is spent in classrooms getting students to read on grade level that little time is left to focus on writing skills. To help teachers include more writing in their daily literacy instruction, each section of this guide has a literature-based reader response prompt. Each of the three genres of writing is used in the reader responses within this guide: narrative, informative/explanatory, and opinion. Before students write, you may want to allow them time to draw pictures related to the topic. Book-themed writing paper is provided on page 70 if your students need more space to write.

Guided Close Reading

Within each section of this guide, it is suggested that you closely reread a portion of the text with your students. Page numbers are given, but since some versions of the books may have different page numbers, the sections to be reread are described by location as well. After rereading the section, there are a few text-dependent questions to be answered by students. Working space has been provided to help students prepare for the group discussion. They should record their thoughts and ideas on the activity page and refer to it during your discussion. If your students are working above grade level, you may want to encourage them to respond to the questions in complete sentences.

Encourage students to read one question at a time and then go back to the text and discover the answer. Work with students to ensure that they use the text to determine their answers rather than making unsupported inferences. Suggested answers are provided in the answer key.

How to Use This Literature Guide (cont.)

Guided Close Reading (cont.)

The generic open-ended stems below can be used to write your own text-dependent questions if you would like to give students more practice.

- ¿Qué palabras del cuento respaldan...?
- ¿Qué texto te ayuda a entender...?
- Usa el libro para explicar por qué sucedió...
- Basándote en los sucesos del cuento, ¿...?
- Muéstrame la parte del texto que apoya...
- Usa el texto para explicar por qué...

Making Connections

The activities in this section help students make cross-curricular connections to mathematics, science, social studies, fine arts, or other curricular areas. These activities require higher-order thinking skills from students but also allow for creative thinking.

Language Learning

A special section has been set aside to connect the literature to language conventions. Through these activities, students will have opportunities to practice the conventions of standard English grammar, usage, capitalization, and punctuation.

Story Elements

It is important to spend time discussing what the common story elements are in literature. Understanding the characters, setting, plot, and theme can increase students' comprehension and appreciation of the story. If teachers begin discussing these elements in early childhood, students will more likely internalize the concepts and look for the elements in their independent reading. Another very important reason for focusing on the story elements is that students will be better writers if they think about how the stories they read are constructed.

In the story elements activities, students are asked to create work related to the characters, setting, or plot. Consider having students complete only one of these activities. If you give students a choice on this assignment, each student can decide to complete the activity that most appeals to him or her. Different intelligences are used so that the activities are diverse and interesting to all students.

How to Use This Literature Guide (cont.)

Culminating Activity

At the end of this instructional guide is a creative culminating activity that allows students the opportunity to share what they've learned from reading the book. This activity is open ended so that students can push themselves to create their own great works within your language arts classroom.

Comprehension Assessment

The questions in this section require students to think about the book they've read as well as the words that were used in the book. Some questions are tied to quotations from the book to engage students and require them to think about the text as they answer the questions.

Response to Literature

Finally, students are asked to respond to the literature by drawing pictures and writing about the characters and stories. A suggested rubric is provided for teacher reference.

Correlation to the Standards

Shell Education is committed to producing educational materials that are research and standards based. As part of this effort, we have correlated all of our products to the academic standards of all 50 states, the District of Columbia, the Department of Defense Dependents Schools, and all Canadian provinces.

Purpose and Intent of Standards

Standards are designed to focus instruction and guide adoption of curricula. Standards are statements that describe the criteria necessary for students to meet specific academic goals. They define the knowledge, skills, and content students should acquire at each level. Standards are also used to develop standardized tests to evaluate students' academic progress. Teachers are required to demonstrate how their lessons meet standards. Standards are used in the development of all of our products, so educators can be assured they meet high academic standards.

How To Find Standards Correlations

To print a customized correlation report of this product for your state, visit our website at http://www.shelleducation.com and follow the online directions. If you require assistance in printing correlation reports, please contact our Customer Service Department at 1-877-777-3450.

Correlation to the Standards (cont.)

Standards Correlation Chart

The lessons in this guide were written to support today's college and career readiness standards. The following chart indicates which sections of this guide address each standard.

College and Career Readiness Standard	Section
Read closely to determine what the text says explicitly and to make logical inferences from it; cite specific textual evidence when writing or speaking to support conclusions drawn from the text.	Analyzing the Literature Sections 1–4; Guided Close Reading Sections 1–4; Story Elements Sections 1–4
Determine central ideas or themes of a text and analyze their development; summarize the key supporting details and ideas.	Analyzing the Literature Sections 1–4; Guided Close Reading Sections 1–4; Making Connections Section 4; Post-Reading Response to Literature; Culminating Activity
Analyze how and why individuals, events, or ideas develop and interact over the course of a text.	Analyzing the Literature Sections 1–4; Guided Close Reading Sections 1–4; Story Elements Sections 1–4; Post-Reading Response to Literature
Interpret words and phrases as they are used in a text, including determining technical, connotative, and figurative meanings, and analyze how specific word choices shape meaning or tone.	Vocabulary Sections 1–4; Making Connections Sections 1, 3
Analyze the structure of texts, including how specific sentences, paragraphs, and larger portions of the text relate to each other and the whole.	Post-Reading Theme Thoughts
Integrate and evaluate content presented in diverse media and formats, including visually and quantitatively, as well as in words.	Pre-Reading Activities; Story Elements Section 1
Read and comprehend complex literary and informational texts independently and proficiently.	Entire Unit
Write arguments to support claims in an analysis of substantive topics or texts using valid reasoning and relevant and sufficient evidence.	Reader Response Section 4

Introduction

Correlation to the Standards (cont.)

Standards Correlation Chart (cont.)

College and Career Readiness Standard	Section
Write informative/explanatory texts to examine and convey complex ideas and information clearly and accurately through the effective selection, organization, and analysis of content	Reader Response Section 2
Write narratives to develop real or imagined experiences or events using effective technique, well-chosen details and well-structured event sequences.	Reader Response Sections 1, 3; Story Elements Section 4
Demonstrate command of the conventions of standard English grammar and usage when writing or speaking.	Language Learning Sections 1, 3
Demonstrate command of the conventions of standard English capitalization, punctuation, and spelling when writing.	Language Learning Sections 2, 4; Reader Response Sections 1–4; Story Elements Sections 1, 3–4
Determine or clarify the meaning of unknown and multiple-meaning words and phrases by using context clues, analyzing meaningful word parts, and consulting general and specialized reference materials, as appropriate.	Vocabulary Sections 1–4
Acquire and use accurately a range of general academic and domain-specific words and phrases sufficient for reading, writing, speaking, and listening at the college and career readiness level; demonstrate independence in gathering vocabulary knowledge when encountering an unknown term important to comprehension or expression.	Vocabulary Sections 1–4

Introduction

About the Author—P.D. Eastman

Philip Dey Eastman was born on November 25, 1909, in Amherst, Massachusetts. He is better known by his pen name, P.D. Eastman. Little is known about his childhood, but it is known that he attended and graduated from Amherst College as well as the National Academy of Design in New York City. After college, Eastman moved to Los Angeles. His early career included art jobs at Walt Disney Productions and Warner Brothers. Eastman married Mary Louise Whitham in 1941.

In 1943, Eastman joined the army. His job assignment was with the Signal Corps Film unit. Theodor Seuss Geisel (later known by the pen name Dr. Seuss) was the head of the film unit, and under Geisel's direction, Eastman worked as a writer and storyboard artist for army training films.

After the army, Eastman worked at United Productions of America (UPA) as a writer and storyboard artist. He worked on the cartoon *Mr. Magoo*. Eastman also helped adapt the children's record *Gerald McBoing Boing* by Theodor Geisel into a short film.

In 1954, Eastman, his wife, and two sons moved from Los Angeles to Westport, Connecticut, where he continued his art career doing freelance work. His career in books began when Theodor Geisel asked him to write for a new series of Beginner Books for Random House.

Eastman died on January 7, 1986. Before his death, he had written or illustrated many favorite books, including: *Are You My Mother?*, *Go, Dog, Go!*, *The Best Nest*, and *Fish Out of Water*.

Possible Texts for Text Comparisons

Although *Are You My Mother?* is not a book in a series, there are several other books by P.D. Eastman with birds as characters. These books make for excellent comparisons of texts by the same author: *Flap Your Wings*, *The Best Nest*, and *My Nest Is Best* (based on *The Best Nest*).

Cross-Curricular Connection

This book can be used in a science unit about animals as students begin to understand the characteristics of birds and that animals closely resemble their parents. In social studies, this book can be used as part of a unit on families.

Introduction

Book Summary of *Are You My Mother?*

Babies need someone to love them, even baby birds. P.D. Eastman tells what happens to a baby bird that cannot find his mother. In the story, a mother bird can tell that the egg she has been sitting on is about to hatch, so she goes to find food for the baby. While she is gone, the egg hatches.

The newly hatched baby bird desperately looks for his mother. As he does, he falls out of the nest and tree. He cannot fly yet, so he sets out walking to look for his mother. The baby is not wise to the world yet, so he approaches anyone and anything to try to find his mother, including a dog, a cow, and a boat. As he searches, he unknowingly passes his mother.

The baby bird finally comes to a large scooper truck, which he calls a Snort. When the baby asks the Snort if it is his mother, the Snort scoops up the baby bird and gently sets him back in his nest in the tree. The baby is safe at home. The mother bird returns with a worm, and the baby bird is happy to have his mother back with him.

Possible Texts for Text Sets

- Garelick, May. *What Makes a Bird a Bird?* Mondo Pub, 1995.
- Jenkins, Priscilla Belz. *A Nest Full of Eggs*. HarperCollins, 1995.
- Rabe, Tish. *Fine Feathered Friends: All About Birds*. Random House Books for Young Readers, 1998.
- Sill, Cathryn. *About Birds: A Guide for Children*. Peachtree Publishers, 2013.

or

- Graves, Keith. *Chicken Big*. Chronicle Books, 2014.
- Guarino, Deborah. *Is Your Mama a Llama?* Scholastic, 1997.
- Kasza, Keiko. *A Mother for Choco*. Puffin, 1996.
- Robbins, Maria Polushkin. *Mother, Mother, I Want Another*. Dragonfly Books, 2007.

Nombre _____

Introducción

Prelectura: pensamientos sobre el tema

Instrucciones: Dibuja una carita feliz o una carita triste. La carita debe mostrar qué piensas de cada afirmación. Luego, usa palabras para explicar qué piensas de cada afirmación.

Afirmación	¿Qué piensas? 😊 ☹	Explica tu respuesta.
Las mamás cuidan de sus bebés.		
Los bebés necesitan a sus mamás.		
Las aventuras siempre son divertidas y emocionantes.		
Solo pasan cosas malas cuando tienes miedo.		

Teacher Plans—Section 1
Pre-Reading

Pre-Reading Activities

Previewing the Cover

1. Display the cover of *Are You My Mother?* Read the title and the author's name. Explain that when an illustrator is not listed, it usually means the author also illustrated the book.

2. Point out the "I Can Read It All By Myself—Beginner Books" icon in the upper right-hand corner. Ask students if they can identify the character shown in the icon. You may want to share with students some background on P.D. Eastman and his connection with Dr. Seuss at this point. (See page 11 for further information.)

3. Point out the question mark in the title. Explain that the words in the title ask a question. Have students look at the illustration and discuss what they see. Ask students to predict who is asking the question and to whom it is being asked. Have students provide reasons supported by the cover illustration for the characters they name.

Previewing the Book

1. Take a picture walk through the book to allow students to look at all the illustrations. Pause at various points in the book to discuss what students have seen and to allow them to make predictions.

2. Based on the picture walk, ask students to identify if the book is fiction or nonfiction and how they know.

Making Personal Connections

1. Confirm students' predictions that the bird is asking the question in the title, and provide reasons. For example, the bird looks like he is talking because his mouth is open and the dog does not look like he is looking for anything since he is laying on the ground.

2. Explain to students that the bird is asking the question, "Are You My Mother?" because he gets separated from his mother. Ask students to tell about a time when they have been separated from their parents, for example: lost in a store, separated by a business trip, or simply apart during school hours.

3. Have students share ways they coped with being separated from their parents.

Teacher Plans—Section 1
Pages 1-17

Vocabulary Overview

Key words and phrases from this section are provided below with definitions and sentences about how the words are used in the story. Introduce and discuss these important vocabulary words with students. If you think these words or other words in the story warrant more time devoted to them, there are suggestions in the introduction for other vocabulary activities (page 5).

Palabra o frase	Definición	Oración sobre el texto
escrito (title page)	hecho con palabras	El cuento fue **escrito** por P.D. Eastman.
ilustrado (title page)	hecho con dibujos	El cuento fue **ilustrado** por P.D. Eastman.
mamá (pg. 3)	una madre	La **mamá** pájara cuida de su huevo.
pájaro (pg. 3)	un animal vertebrado de sangre caliente con plumas y alas	La mamá **pájara** pone un huevo.
huevo (pg. 3)	un objeto ovalado con cáscara dura que eclosiona para que de él nazca un pajarito	La mamá pájara pone un **huevo**.
de repente (pg. 3)	inesperadamente; súbitamente	**De repente**, el huevo se movió.
del (pg. 9)	desde el centro	Un pajarito sale **del** huevo.
hacia (pg. 12)	en dirección a	El pajarito mira **hacia** arriba.
arriba (pg. 12)	en posición más alta	El pajarito mira hacia **arriba**.
abajo (pg. 18)	en posición más baja	El pajarito mira hacia **abajo**.

Páginas 1–17

Nombre _____

Actividad del vocabulario

Instrucciones: Cada imagen muestra una pelota y una caja. Debajo de cada imagen escribe la palabra del banco de palabras que **mejor** indica la ubicación o el movimiento de la pelota.

Banco de palabras

| hacia | arriba | abajo | del |

Teacher Plans—Section 1
Pages 1-17

Analyzing the Literature

Provided below are discussion questions you can use in small groups, with the whole class, or for written assignments. Each question is written at two levels so you can choose the right question for each group of students. For each question, a few key points are provided for your reference as you discuss the book with students.

Story Element	Level 1 Questions for Students	Level 2 Questions for Students	Key Discussion Points
Character	¿Quiénes son los personajes del cuento?	Describe cómo se presenta cada personaje en el cuento.	The characters are a mother bird and her newly hatched baby bird. The mother bird is introduced sitting on her egg in the nest. The baby bird is shown hatching out of the egg.
Setting	Describe el escenario que se muestra en las ilustraciones.	¿Qué palabras describen el escenario?	The setting is not explicitly stated and very little background is provided in the illustrations, except for the tree, the nest in the tree, and grass. The illustrations show that the setting is clearly outdoors. The text and illustrations support that the baby bird falls out of the tree, walks on the ground, and begins his search.
Plot	¿Qué es lo primero que hace el bebé cuando nace?	Describe cuándo el bebé empieza a buscar a su mamá.	The baby bird asks for his mother. The baby bird does not see his mother, so he immediately begins to look all around for her. The text says he knows he has a mother, so he goes to find her.

© Shell Education   51749—Instructional Guide: ¿Eres tú mi mamá?   17

Páginas 1-17

Nombre _____

Reflexión del lector

Piensa

En este cuento, el pajarito es separado de su mamá. Piensa en alguna vez que hayas sido separado de alguien querido.

Tema de escritura narrativa

Escribe sobre alguna vez que te hayas perdido o te hayas separado de alguien querido. Di lo que pasó.

Nombre _____

Páginas 1–17

Lectura enfocada guiada

Vuelve a leer con atención las páginas que describen cómo se va volando la mamá pájara (páginas 3–7).

Instrucciones: Piensa en estas preguntas. En los espacios, escribe ideas o haz dibujos. Prepárate para compartir tus respuestas.

❶ ¿Cómo sabes que la mamá pájara sabe que el huevo eclosionará pronto?

❷ ¿Qué palabras explican por qué la mamá pájara deja solo el huevo?

❸ ¿Es buena mamá la mamá pájara o no? Usa evidencia para apoyar tu respuesta.

Páginas 1-17

Nombre _____

Relacionarse: una buena mamá

Instrucciones: Colorea las palabras de abajo que describen a una buena mamá. Traza una *X* en las palabras que no describen a una buena mamá. Luego usa algunas palabras coloreadas para escribir sobre una buena mamá que conozcas.

cariñosa	mimosa	dura	severa
deja de lado	servicial	atenta	apegada
odiosa	besucona	egoísta	dulce

_____
_____
_____
_____
_____
_____

Nombre _____

Páginas 1–17

Relacionarse: ciencia

Instrucciones: Lee sobre los pájaros. Luego usa las palabras del banco de palabras para nombrar cada pájaro de abajo.

Los pájaros son animales con plumas y alas. La mayoría de los pájaros pueden volar. Los pájaros ponen huevos. La mamá pájara se sienta sobre el huevo para mantenerlo cálido. El huevo eclosiona y sale un bebé pájaro.

Banco de palabras

búho	pingüino	flamenco
avestruz	colibrí	cuervo

1. _____

2. _____

3. _____

4. _____

5. _____

6. _____

Aprendizaje del lenguaje: sustantivos y verbos

Instrucciones: Los *sustantivos* son palabras que nombran personas, lugares y cosas. Los *verbos* son palabras que representan acciones. Muestran lo que ocurre. Recorta las tarjetas de la parte de abajo de la hoja. Pega cada palabra en la columna correcta para mostrar si es un sustantivo o un verbo.

Sustantivos: palabras para nombrar	Verbos: palabras que representan acciones

huevo	caminar	volar	saltar	bebé
comer	mamá	mirar	pájaro	árbol

Nombre _____

Páginas 1–17

Elementos del texto: personajes

Instrucciones: Escoge a la mamá **O** al bebé. Dibuja la cara del pájaro para mostrar cómo se siente en cada uno de los momentos.

Mamá pájara	Pajarito
1. cuando empolla su huevo	1. dentro del huevo
2. cuando se mueve el huevo	2. cuando sale del huevo
3. cuando piensa en qué necesitará	3. cuando no puede hallar a su mamá
4. cuando se va del nido	4. cuando empieza a buscarla

1.

2.

3.

4.

Páginas 1–17

Nombre _____

Elementos del texto: escenario

Instrucciones: Dibuja o pinta el escenario. Solo incluye los detalles que se muestran en las ilustraciones del libro. Escribe una oración que describa el escenario.

Nombre _____

Páginas 1–17

Elementos del texto: trama

Instrucciones: Escríbele una carta a un amigo. En tu carta, predice qué ocurrirá después de que el pajarito llega al suelo.

_____

Querido _____ :

_____

_____

_____

_____

_____

_____

De parte de,

_____

_____

Teacher Plans—Section 2
Pages 18–37

Vocabulary Overview

Key words and phrases from this section are provided below with definitions and sentences about how the words are used in the story. Introduce and discuss these important vocabulary words with students. If you think these words or other words in the story warrant more time devoted to them, there are suggestions in the introduction for other vocabulary activities (page 5).

Palabra o frase	Definición	Oración sobre el texto
volar (pg. 18)	moverse por el aire	El pajarito no sabe **volar**.
buscar (pg. 19)	hacer algo para encontrar a alguien o algo	El pajarito sale a **buscar** a su mamá.
cerca (pg. 20)	no lejos	El pajarito pasa muy **cerca** de su mamá.
gatito (pg. 22)	un gato bebé	El pajarito habla con el **gatito**.
no decía nada (pg. 23)	no hablar o no responder	El gatito **no decía nada**.
siguió (pg. 24)	continuó	El pajarito **siguió** su camino.
gallina (pg. 25)	un ave de granja que se come	El pajarito habla con la **gallina**.
perro (pg. 28)	un mamífero relacionado con los lobos, que puede ser mascota	El pajarito habla con el **perro**.
vaca (pg. 31)	un animal bovino que se encuentra en una granja	El pajarito habla con la **vaca**.

Nombre _____

Páginas 18-37

Actividad del vocabulario

Instrucciones: Escoge dos palabras del vocabulario. Escribe una oración para cada una. Asegúrate de que las oraciones muestren lo que significan las palabras.

Palabras del cuento

volar	buscar	gatito
gallina	perro	vaca

Palabra	Oración

Instrucciones: Contesta esta pregunta.

1. Después de hablar con cada animal, el bebé **siguió**. ¿Por qué?

_____
_____
_____
_____

Teacher Plans—Section 2
Pages 18-37

Analyzing the Literature

Provided below are discussion questions you can use in small groups, with the whole class, or for written assignments. Each question is written at two levels so you can choose the right question for each group of students. For each question, a few key points are provided for your reference as you discuss the book with students.

Story Element	Level 1 Questions for Students	Level 2 Questions for Students	Key Discussion Points
Character	¿Quiénes son los nuevos personajes de esta sección?	¿Por qué habla con diferentes animales el pajarito?	A kitten, hen, dog, and cow are introduced in this section. The baby bird asks each animal if it is his mother as the baby bird continues to search for his mother.
Setting	¿De qué forma las ilustraciones muestran el escenario de esta sección?	¿Cómo aprendes acerca del escenario de este cuento?	The text does not explicitly state a setting and the illustrations provide limited details. The setting is outdoors, and it can be inferred that the setting is away from a city, probably the country due to the types of animals the baby bird talks to—a kitten, hen, dog, and cow.
Plot	¿Por qué sigue buscando a su mamá después de hablar con cada animal el pajarito?	¿Qué evidencia hay de que el pajarito está decidido a encontrar a su mamá?	The baby bird continues to search for the mother, even when he cannot find her. He states, "I have to find my mother!" The capital letters in the words the second time they are stated show emphasis and his determination to find his mother.

Nombre _____

Páginas 18-37

Reflexión del lector

Piensa

Piensa en el hecho de que el pajarito pasa muy cerca de su mamá y no la ve ni la reconoce.

Tema de escritura informativa/explicativa

Escribe sobre la apariencia de los pájaros. Provee datos sobre cómo se ven y cómo actúan los pájaros.

Lectura enfocada guiada

Vuelve a leer con atención la parte donde el pajarito pasa muy cerca de su mamá (páginas 20–21).

Instrucciones: Piensa en estas preguntas. En los espacios, escribe ideas o haz dibujos. Prepárate para compartir tus respuestas.

❶ Basándote en el cuento, ¿por qué pasa muy cerca de su mamá y sin embargo sigue su camino el pajarito?

❷ ¿Qué texto le ayuda al lector a entender por qué el bebé les pregunta a diferentes animales si son su mamá?

❸ ¿Qué dicen las ilustraciones sobre la mamá?

Nombre _____

Páginas 18-37

Relacionarse: dobles

Instrucciones: Muchos bebés animales se parecen a sus papás. Escribe o dibuja razones por las que el pajarito no se parece a cada animal con el que habla.

gatito	**gallina**
perro	**vaca**

Páginas 18–37

Nombre _____

Relacionarse: matemáticas

Instrucciones: El pajarito tiene dos patas. Cuenta cuántas patas habría si hubiera más pajaritos. Escribe tu respuesta en cada casilla.

Ejemplo:

2 + 2 = 4 patas

1. _____ + _____ + _____ + _____ = ☐

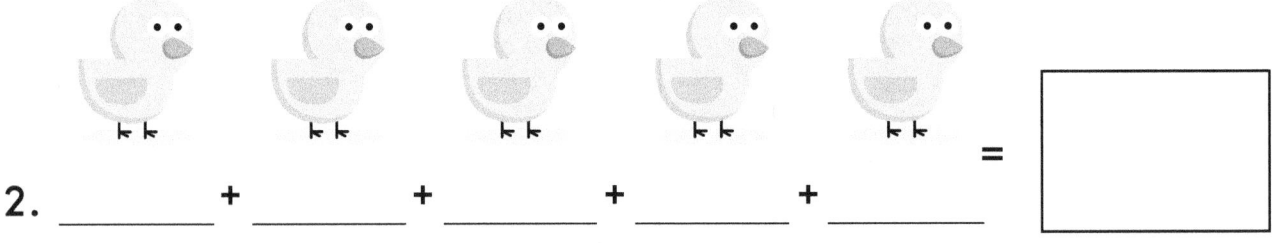

2. _____ + _____ + _____ + _____ + _____ = ☐

3. _____ + _____ + _____ = ☐

Nombre _____

Páginas 18-37

Aprendizaje del lenguaje: preguntas

Instrucciones: Las preguntas son oraciones que preguntan algo. Empiezan y acaban con signos de interrogación. Recorta los signos de interrogación en la parte de abajo y pega uno al principio y al final de cada oración. Estas oraciones están en el libro.

1. ☐ Eres tú mi mamá ☐

2. ☐ Dónde está ☐

3. ☐ Dónde podría estar ☐

4. ☐ Cómo voy a ser yo tu mamá ☐

5. ☐ Tenía mamá ☐

Instrucciones: Encierra la palabra de pregunta al principio de cada oración de arriba. Escoge una de las palabras y escribe tu propia pregunta.

_____

_____

_____

_____

| ¿ | ¿ | ¿ | ¿ | ¿ | | ? | ? | ? | ? | ? |

Páginas 18-37

Nombre _____

Elementos del texto: personajes

Instrucciones: El bebé pájaro le pregunta a cuatro animales si son su mamá. Cada animal le contesta de manera distinta. ¿Qué dice o hace cada animal?

gatito	
gallina	
perro	
vaca	

Nombre _____

Páginas 18-37

Elementos del texto: escenario

Instrucciones: Haz un dibujo de un escenario donde encontrarías un gatito, una gallina, un perro y una vaca. Incluye otros animales que encontrarías en ese escenario. Escribe un título para tu dibujo.

_____

_____

Páginas 18-37

Nombre _____

Elementos del texto: trama

Instrucciones: Dibuja los cuatro animales con los que habla el pajarito. Ponlos en el orden correcto. Escribe el nombre de cada animal en el renglón debajo de las casillas.

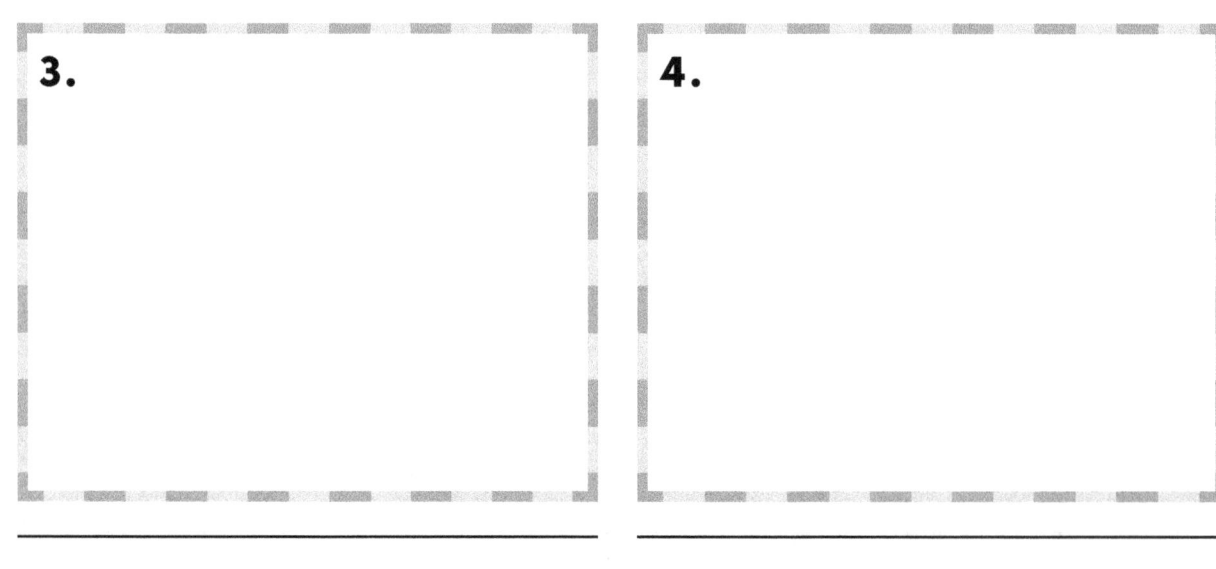

Teacher Plans—Section 3
Pages 38-49

Vocabulary Overview

Key words and phrases from this section are provided below with definitions and sentences about how the words are used in the story. Introduce and discuss these important vocabulary words with students. If you think these words or other words in the story warrant more time devoted to them, there are suggestions in the introduction for other vocabulary activities (page 5).

Palabra o frase	Definición	Oración sobre el texto
corría (pg. 38)	movía las patas a una velocidad más rápida que cuando camina	El pajarito **corría**.
automóvil (pg. 38)	un vehículo con cuatro ruedas usado para viajar	El pajarito ve un **automóvil**.
viejo (pg. 38)	gastado; no nuevo	El automóvil es **viejo**.
se detuvo (pg. 39)	se paró después de haber estado moviéndose	El pajarito no **se detuvo**.
se alejó (pg. 39)	siguió su camino	El pajarito **se alejó**.
barco (pg. 40)	un vehículo usado para viajar sobre el agua	El pajarito ve un **barco**.
avión (pg. 42)	un vehículo con alas usado para viajar por el aire	El pajarito ve un **avión**.
gritó (pg. 42)	habló con voz muy alta	El pajarito **gritó** llamando a su mamá.
máquina (pg. 44)	un aparato	El pajarito ve una **máquina** grande.

Páginas 38-49

Nombre _____

Actividad del vocabulario

Instrucciones: Haz un dibujo para cada palabra del vocabulario.

automóvil	avión
barco	**máquina**

Instrucciones: Contesta esta pregunta.

1. ¿Qué cosa del cuento es **vieja**?

_____

- -

Teacher Plans—Section 3
Pages 38–49

Analyzing the Literature

Provided below are discussion questions you can use in small groups, with the whole class, or for written assignments. Each question is written at two levels so you can choose the right question for each group of students. For each question, a few key points are provided for your reference as you discuss the book with students.

Story Element	Level 1 Questions for Students	Level 2 Questions for Students	Key Discussion Points
Character	¿Cómo intenta comunicarse con los objetos que encuentra el pajarito?	Describe la respuesta de los objetos al pajarito.	The baby bird calls out to the boat, but the boat goes on. Then, the baby bird calls out to the big plane, but the plane goes on. The baby bird talks to the big thing and the big things says, "Snort." The objects do not talk to the baby bird because they are not alive. They just continue with their jobs because they cannot interact with the baby bird.
Setting	Describe los nuevos escenarios que se presentan en esta sección.	Hay más detalle en las ilustraciones que antes en el libro. Describe en qué consiste la diferencia.	The settings show a yard with a broken-down car, a river, the air, and a construction site. In the end, the baby bird is returned to his nest in the tree. Although the background illustrations are still sparse, there is more detail in what is shown.
Plot	Describe los otros objetos con los que se encuentra el pajarito mientras busca a su mamá.	¿Cómo te ayudan las ilustraciones a entender los otros objetos con los que se encuentra el pajarito mientras busca a su mamá?	The baby bird comes across a car, a boat, a plane, and a front-loader. The boat and the plane keep moving on. The illustrations clearly show all of these vehicles. The illustrations show these vehicles in their settings and help the reader to understand what a boat, plane, and front-loader are.

Páginas 38–49

Nombre _____

Reflexión del lector

Piensa

Piensa en la búsqueda del pajarito de su mamá. Se encuentra con muchos tipos de transporte, como un automóvil, un barco y un avión.

Tema de escritura narrativa

Escribe sobre las diferentes cosas que ves cuando vas camino a la escuela.

Nombre _____

Páginas 38-49

Lectura enfocada guiada

Vuelve a leer con atención la parte donde el pajarito primero interactúa con la máquina (páginas 46–49).

Instrucciones: Piensa en estas preguntas. En los espacios, escribe ideas o haz dibujos. Prepárate para compartir tus respuestas.

❶ Basándote en el cuento, ¿por qué crees que el pajarito podría pensar que la máquina grande es su mamá?

❷ ¿Qué hizo la máquina?

❸ ¿Qué evidencia hay de que el pajarito tiene miedo de la máquina?

Páginas 38-49

Nombre _____

Relacionarse: pájaros y aviones

Instrucciones: El pajarito es parecido a un avión. Piensa en todas las maneras en las que los pájaros y los aviones se parecen y se diferencian. Dibuja y escribe en este diagrama de Venn.

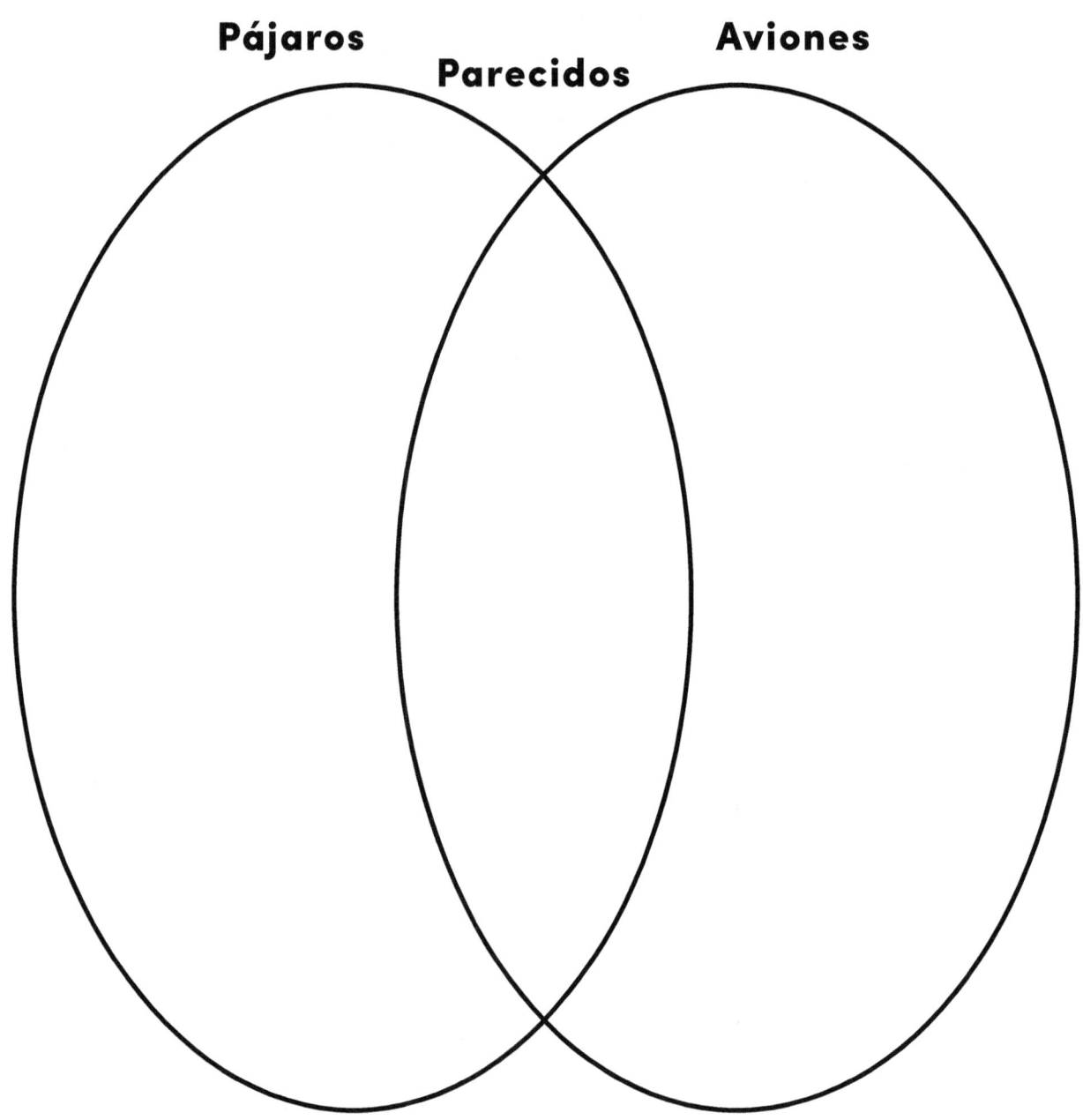

Nombre _____

Páginas 38-49

Relacionarse: ciencias sociales

Instrucciones: Hay distintos tipos de transporte en esta sección del cuento. Recorta cada objeto de abajo y pégalo en la columna correcta.

Tierra	Agua	Aire

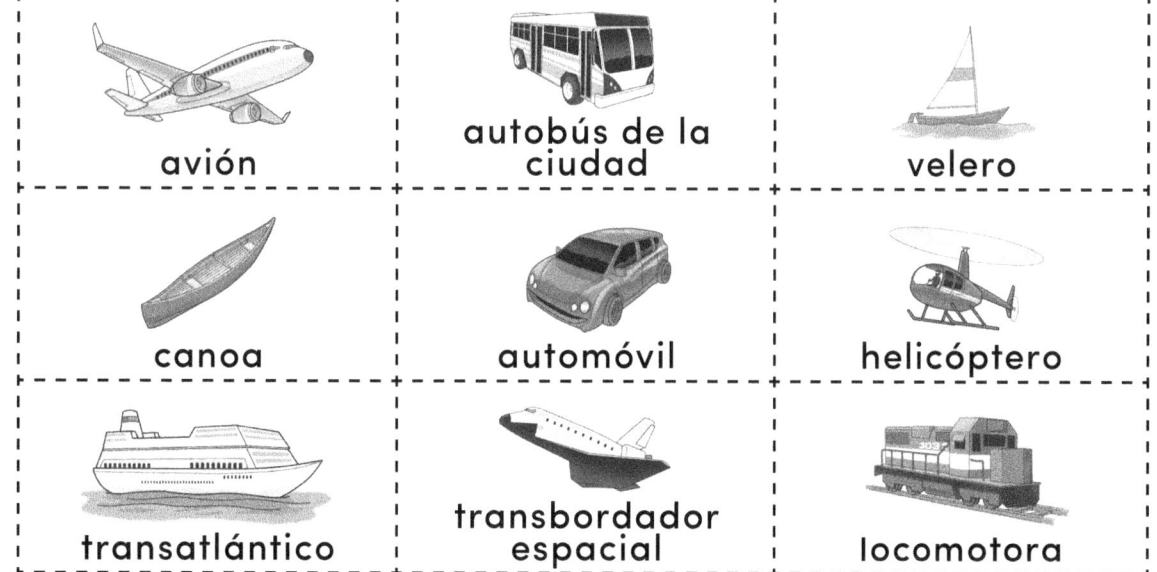

avión | autobús de la ciudad | velero

canoa | automóvil | helicóptero

transatlántico | transbordador espacial | locomotora

Páginas 38-49

Nombre _____

Aprendizaje del lenguaje: adjetivos

Instrucciones: Los adjetivos describen a los sustantivos. Escribe algunos adjetivos para describir estos objetos del libro.

Objeto del cuento	Adjetivos

Nombre _____

Páginas 38-49

Elementos del texto: personajes

Instrucciones: La máquina grande hace "PUFFF". Escribe lo que el automóvil, el barco y el avión dirían si pudieran hablar.

Páginas 38-49

Nombre _____

Elementos del texto: trama

Instrucciones: Escoge otro objeto con el que podría hablar el pajarito. Escribe un diálogo entre el pajarito y esta otra "mamá".

"

                    ", dice el pajarito.

Dice   :

"   "
                                        .

El pajarito dice: "
                                        "
                                        .

"

                              ", responde.

Nombre _____

Páginas 38-49

Elementos del texto: escenario

Instrucciones: Haz un dibujo de tu escenario favorito de esta sección del cuento. Asegúrate de incluir muchos detalles en tu dibujo.

Teacher Plans—Section 4
Pages 50-64

Vocabulary Overview

Key words and phrases from this section are provided below with definitions and sentences about how the words are used in the story. Introduce and discuss these important vocabulary words with students. If you think these words or other words in the story warrant more time devoted to them, there are suggestions in the introduction for other vocabulary activities (page 5).

Palabra o frase	Definición	Oración sobre el texto
muy alto (pg. 50)	elevado	La máquina subió **muy alto**.
en ese momento (pg. 55)	un momento específico en el pasado	**En ese momento**, se detuvo.
sucedió (pg. 59)	ocurrió	Algo **sucedió**.
casa (pg. 59)	el lugar donde vive una persona o un animal	El árbol es la **casa** del pajarito.
árbol (pg. 59)	una planta alta y leñosa	Regresaron el pajarito al **árbol**.
preciso (pg. 60)	exacto	En ese **preciso** momento, su mamá regresó.
regresó (pg. 60)	volvió	La mamá **regresó**.
sabes (pg. 60)	reconoces a alguien o algo	¿**Sabes** quién soy yo?

Nombre _____

Páginas 50-64

Actividad del vocabulario

Instrucciones: Completa cada oración de abajo. Usa una de las palabras o frases a continuación.

Palabras y frases del cuento

muy alto	en ese momento	casa	sucedió
preciso	árbol	regresó	sabes

1. La máquina sube _____.

2. La máquina devuelve el pajarito al _____.

3. El pajarito está en su _____.

4. _____, su mamá regresa al árbol.

Instrucciones: Contesta esta pregunta.

5. ¿Qué **sabe** el pajarito entonces?

_____

_____

_____

Teacher Plans—Section 4
Pages 50-64

Analyzing the Literature

Provided below are discussion questions you can use in small groups, with the whole class, or for written assignments. Each question is written at two levels so you can choose the right question for each group of students. For each question, a few key points are provided for your reference as you discuss the book with students.

Story Element	Level 1 Questions for Students	Level 2 Questions for Students	Key Discussion Points
Character	¿Qué le dice el pajarito a su mamá cuando se ven?	Describe cómo se siente el pajarito cuando ve a su mamá.	The baby bird says, "I know who you are." The baby bird then goes on to say all the things the mother is not. Then, the baby bird says, "You are a bird, and you are my mother." The baby bird is very happy, and the illustrations show that.
Setting	Describe el escenario que se muestra en las ilustraciones.	¿Qué palabras describen el escenario?	The setting is a field with a front-loader in the dirt and a nest in a tree. The text and illustrations support that the baby bird is helped by the Snort and put back into the nest in the tree.
Plot	¿Cómo ayuda la máquina al pajarito?	¿Qué puedes deducir sobre por qué la máquina ayuda al pajarito?	Although the Snort is not alive, it must have a person in it to drive it. The person must have seen the baby bird and decided to help the baby bird get back into the nest in the tree.

Nombre _____

Páginas 50-64

Reflexión del lector

Piensa

La mamá pájara se ha ido del nido cuando nace el bebé y después regresa al nido y a su bebé. Piensa en si la mamá pájara es una buena mamá o no.

Tema de escritura de opinión

Escribe tu opinión sobre si piensas que la mamá pájara es buena mamá o no. Asegúrate de dar razones para apoyar tu opinión.

Páginas 50-64

Nombre _____

Lectura enfocada guiada

Vuelve a leer con atención cuando el pajarito está encima de la máquina (páginas 52–57).

Instrucciones: Piensa en estas preguntas. En los espacios, escribe ideas o haz dibujos. Prepárate para compartir tus respuestas.

❶ Usa el libro para contar lo que quiere el pajarito.

❷ ¿Qué palabras muestran que el pajarito tiene miedo?

❸ Vuelve al texto para ver lo que hace la máquina.

Nombre _____

Páginas 50-64

Relacionarse: hogar dulce hogar

Instrucciones: Al pajarito lo devuelven a su casa. Dibuja y rotula la casa del pajarito. Dibuja y rotula tu casa.

La casa del pajarito

Tu casa

Páginas 50-64

Nombre _____

Relacionarse: ciencias sociales

Instrucciones: La mamá pájara y el pajarito son una familia. Escribe el nombre de las personas de tu familia.

mamá	hermano(s)
papá	hermana(s)
otro	

Instrucciones: Haz un dibujo de tu familia.

Nombre _____

Páginas 50-64

Aprendizaje del lenguaje: orden alfabético

Instrucciones: En este cuento, el pajarito descubre que muchos animales y muchas cosas no son su mamá. Vuelve a escribir la lista de estas cosas en orden alfabético.

Palabras de esta sección	Escríbelas en orden alfabético
perro	_____
gatito	_____
gallina	_____
vaca	_____
avión	_____
barco	_____

ABCDEFGHIJKLMNOPQRSTUVWXYZ

Páginas 50-64

Nombre _____

Elementos del texto: escenario

Instrucciones: Al pajarito lo devuelven a su casa: el nido. Haz un dibujo del pájaro después de que crece y tiene su propio pajarito. Asegúrate de incluir un árbol y un nido con la familia de pájaros.

Nombre _____

Páginas 50-64

Elementos del texto: trama

Instrucciones: Recorta las tarjetas de abajo. Pégalas en otro pedazo de papel en el orden del cuento.

El pajarito sube muy alto en la máquina.

Dice el pajarito: "¡Quiero estar con mi mamá!".

La máquina devuelve el pajarito al nido.

La mamá pájara regresa.

Páginas 50–64

Nombre _____

Elementos del texto: personajes

Instrucciones: Escribe un poema sobre cómo ha cambiado el pajarito desde el principio del cuento hasta el final.

Me pregunté ? ? ?

Cuando estuve dentro del huevo, me pregunté...
_____
_____ .

Cuando salí del huevo, me pregunté...
_____
_____ .

Cuando no pude encontrar a mi mamá, me pregunté...
_____
_____ .

Cuando la máquina me alzó, me pregunté...
_____
_____ .

Cuando regresó mi mamá, supe...
_____
_____ .

Nombre _____

Actividades de la poslectura

Poslectura: pensamientos sobre el tema

Instrucciones: Elige un personaje principal de *¿Eres tú mi mamá?* Imagina que eres ese personaje. Dibuja una carita feliz o una carita triste para mostrar qué piensa el personaje de cada afirmación. Luego, usa palabras para aclarar tu dibujo.

El personaje que elegí _____

Afirmación	¿Qué piensa el personaje? ☺ ☹	Explica tu respuesta
Las mamás cuidan de sus bebés.		
Los bebés necesitan a sus mamás.		
Las aventuras siempre son divertidas y emocionantes.		
Solo pasan cosas malas cuando tienes miedo.		

Post-Reading Activities

Culminating Activity: Home, Sweet Home!

Recreate a nest and the baby bird with these art projects. Directions for each are provided below. Display the nests and baby birds on a bulletin board with the title *Home, Sweet Home!*

Nest Art Project

Materials
- *Nest Pattern* (page 61)
- glue
- brown scrap construction paper
- brown scrap yarn

Directions
1. Copy the *Nest Pattern* on page 61. Have students cut out the pattern.
2. Provide scrap construction paper and yarn in shades of brown. Have students cut up the construction paper and yarn into little pieces and glue them all over the nest.

Other Options
1. Allow students to go outside on the playground to gather other items from nature to glue to the nest such as grass, vines, or pieces of paper or trash they find.
2. Photocopy the *Nest Pattern* onto brown construction paper and cut out or have students color the pattern.

Bird Art Project

Materials
- 8 ½" x 12" brown construction paper (2 per student)
- scrap yellow, orange, white, and black construction paper

Directions
1. Provide each student with two pieces of brown construction paper.
2. Fold one of the pieces in half so that the construction paper now measures 8 ½" x 6".
3. Trace students' hands on the folded construction paper. Have students cut out their hands so that once cut out, they have two hand prints. These will become the birds' wings.
4. Trace each student's foot on the remaining piece of brown construction paper. Have students cut out their feet. These will become the birds' bodies.
5. Orient the footprint vertically, so the heel of the footprint is at the bottom. The head is where the ball of the foot is. Glue the wings on either side of the birds' bodies.
6. Use scrap paper to cut out two feet, two eyes, and a beak. Glue the feet, eyes, and beaks to the birds' body.

Culminating Activity: Nest Pattern

Directions: Copy the pattern. Use the pattern with the nest art project described on page 60.

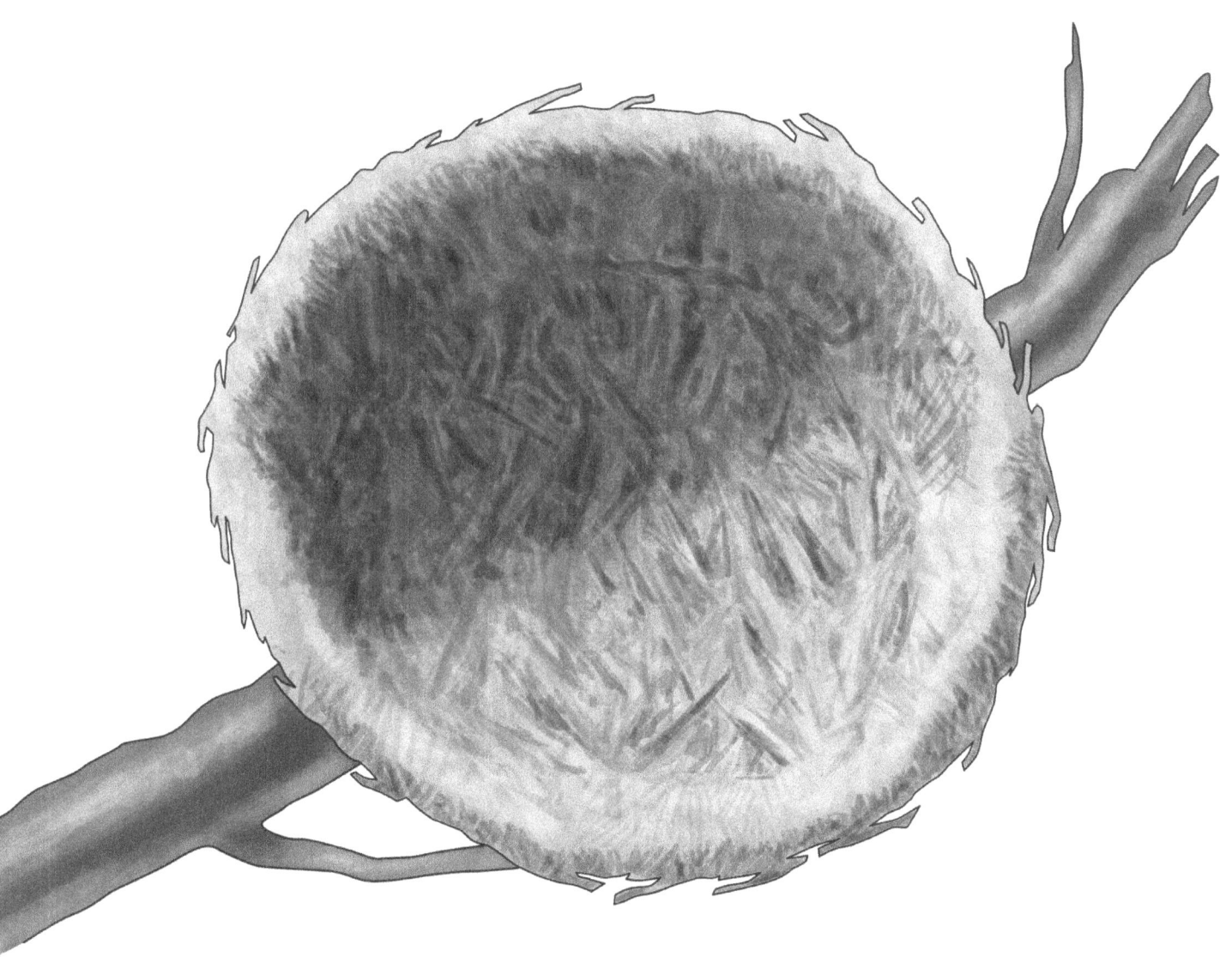

Post-Reading Activities

Culminating Activity: Retelling the Story

Directions: Reproduce the stick puppet patterns on pages 62–64 on tagboard or construction paper. Have students cut them along the dashed lines. To complete the stick puppets, glue each pattern to a tongue depressor or craft stick.

Follow the sequence below to practice retelling the story.

1. Emphasize with students the following attributes of a good retelling:
    - Include the names of the characters.
    - Include the setting.
    - Include the events that happen in the correct sequence.

2. Model what a good retelling sounds like for students. Use the puppets as you retell the story so students see how the puppets help you remember the characters and the sequence of events.

3. Place students with partners. Assist students in lining up their puppets in the order they will use them when retelling the story.

4. Have students practice retelling the story to their partners. Encourage students to help each other if an event needs to be included in the sequence of the retelling.

62 51749—Instructional Guide: ¿Eres tú mi mamá? © Shell Education

Post-Reading Activities

Culminating Activity: Retelling the Story (cont.)

Post-Reading Activities

Culminating Activity: Retelling the Story (cont.)

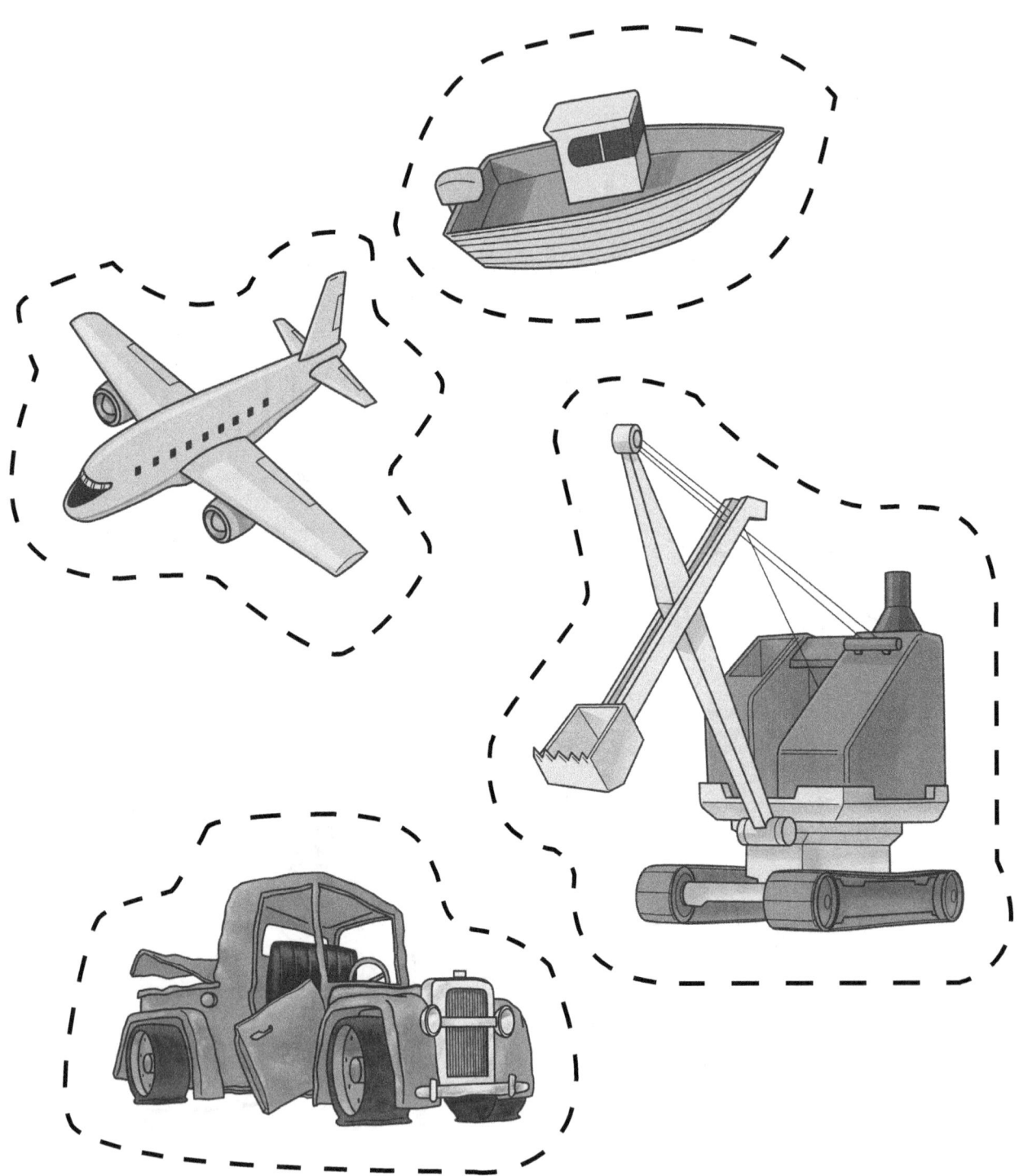

Nombre _____

Actividades de la poslectura

Evaluación de la comprensión

Instrucciones: Rellena la burbuja de la mejor respuesta para cada pregunta.

Sección 1

1. ¿Qué muestra por qué la mamá pájara deja el nido?

   - (A) El huevo salta del nido.
   - (B) El bebé sale del huevo.
   - (C) El pajarito tendrá hambre.
   - (D) Se cansa de estar sentada.

Sección 2

2. ¿Por qué piensa el pajarito que los animales son su mamá?

   - (A) Los animales se parecen al pajarito.
   - (B) Los animales son su mamá.
   - (C) Los animales le hablan al pajarito.
   - (D) El pajarito no conoce el aspecto de su mamá.

Sección 3

3. ¿Qué muestra la forma en la que el pajarito va en busca de su mamá?

   - (A) El barco no se detiene.
   - (B) Él sigue corriendo.
   - (C) Él ve un avión grande.
   - (D) El avión no se detiene.

Actividades de la poslectura

Evaluación de la comprensión (cont.)

Sección 4

4. Describe por qué el pajarito busca a la mamá pájara.

   _____
   _____
   _____
   _____
   _____
   _____

5. ¿Qué oración describe mejor cómo llega a casa el pajarito?

   Ⓐ El pajarito vuela hasta llegar al nido.

   Ⓑ La mamá pájara lo encuentra.

   Ⓒ La máquina devuelve el pajarito al nido.

   Ⓓ El pajarito construye una nueva casa.

Nombre _____

Actividades de la poslectura

Reflexión sobre la literatura: buscando a mamá

Instrucciones: El pajarito piensa que muchos animales y muchas cosas son su mamá. Haz un dibujo de lo que crees que más se parece a su mamá. Luego contesta las preguntas sobre lo que dibujaste en la siguiente página. Asegúrate de que tu dibujo sea claro y esté pintado de colores.

Actividades de la poslectura

Nombre _____

Reflexión sobre la literatura: buscando a mamá (cont.)

1. ¿Qué animal o qué objeto crees que más se parece a la mamá y por qué?
   _____
   _____
   _____

2. ¿Es una buena respuesta la respuesta que da el animal o el objeto al bebé?
   _____
   _____
   _____

3. ¿De qué forma este animal o este objeto podría no ser la mamá del pajarito?
   _____
   _____
   _____

Nombre _____

Actividades de la poslectura

Pauta: Reflexión sobre la literatura

Instrucciones: Use esta pauta para evaluar las respuestas de los estudiantes.

Fantástico trabajo	Bien hecho	Sigue intentándolo
☐ Contestaste las tres preguntas de manera completa. Incluiste muchos detalles.	☐ Contestaste las tres preguntas.	☐ No contestaste las tres preguntas.
☐ Tu caligrafía es fácil de leer. No hay errores de ortografía.	☐ Podrías mejorar tu caligrafía. Hay algunos errores de ortografía.	☐ Tu caligrafía no se puede leer muy fácilmente. Hay muchos errores de ortografía.
☐ Tu dibujo es claro y está coloreado completamente.	☐ Tu dibujo es claro y una parte está coloreada.	☐ Tu dibujo no es muy claro o no está coloreado completamente.
☐ La creatividad es evidente tanto en el dibujo como en el escrito.	☐ La creatividad es evidente en el dibujo o en el escrito.	☐ No hay mucha creatividad ni en el dibujo ni en el escrito.

Comentarios del maestro: _____

_____

_____

_____

Hoja para escribir

Nombre _____

The responses provided here are just examples of what students may answer. Many accurate responses are possible for the questions throughout this unit.

Vocabulary Activity—Section 1 (page 16)
1. arriba
2. hacia
3. del
4. abajo

Guided Close Reading—Section 1 (page 19)
1. "El huevo dio un salto en el nido".
2. "…querrá comer". "¡Voy a buscar algo para darle de comer!".
3. Student answers will vary. Students may argue that the mother is a good mother because she knows her baby will be hungry and is going to get something to eat. Students may argue that the mother is not a good mother because she leaves the egg alone.

Making Connections—Section 1 (page 20)
Students' responses will vary, but the descriptors may include: cariñosa, mimosa, servicial, atenta, apegada, besucona, dulce.

Making Connections—Section 1 (page 21)
1. cuervo
2. pingüino
3. avestruz
4. colibrí
5. búho
6. flamenco

Language Learning—Section 1 (page 22)
- Sustantivos—huevo, pájaro, mamá, bebé, árbol
- Verbos—caminar, saltar, volar, comer, mirar

Vocabulary Activity—Section 2 (page 27)
The vocabulary words students choose will vary. Sentences will vary, too.
1. El pajarito siguió buscando a su mamá.

Guided Close Reading—Section 2 (page 30)
1. El pajarito no conoce el aspecto de su mamá. No la ve.
2. El pajarito no conoce el aspecto de su mamá.
3. La mamá busca comida para el pajarito.

Making Connections—Section 2 (page 31)
Suggested answers are provided below.
- gatito: Un gatito tiene pelo y un pájaro no.
- perro: Un perro tiene cuatro patas y un pájaro no.
- gallina: Una gallina es otro tipo de pájaro.
- vaca: Una vaca es mucho más grande que un pájaro.

Making Connections—Section 2 (page 32)
1. 8 patas
2. 10 patas
3. 6 patas

Language Learning—Section 2 (page 33)
1. Eres
2. Dónde
3. Dónde
4. Cómo
5. Tenía

Story Elements—Section 2 (page 34)
- gatito: solo lo miraba pero no decía nada
- gallina: contestó, "No".
- perro: dijo, "Yo no soy tu mamá. Soy un perro".
- vaca: preguntó, "¿Cómo voy a ser yo tu mamá? ¿No ves que soy una vaca?".

Story Elements—Section 2 (page 35)
Students' pictures should reflect a setting that has a kitten, a hen, a dog, and a cow.

Story Elements—Section 2 (page 36)
The animals should be put in the order listed below and labeled correctly: gatito, gallina, perro, vaca.

Vocabulary Activity—Section 3 (page 38)
Students' illustrations should match the vocabulary words.
1. El texto dice que el automóvil es **viejo**.

Answer Key

Guided Close Reading—Section 3 (page 41)
1. El pajarito no conoce el aspecto de su mamá. Pregunta a muchos animales y a muchas máquinas si son su mamá. El pajarito cree que la máquina es su mamá.
2. La máquina grande hace "PUFFF".
3. El pajarito dice que tiene que irse de allí. La ilustración muestra su cara asustada. Las líneas alrededor de sus alas indican pánico.

Making Connections—Section 3 (page 42)
Students' answers will vary, but should show the similarities and differences of a bird and an airplane.

Making Connections—Section 3 (page 43)

Tierra	Agua	Aire
autobús de la ciudad	canoa	avión
locomotora	velero	helicóptero
automóvil	transatlántico	transbordador espacial

Vocabulary Activity—Section 4 (page 49)
1. La máquina sube **muy alto**.
2. La máquina devuelve el pajarito al **árbol**.
3. El pajarito está en su **casa**.
4. **En ese momento**, su mamá regresa al árbol.
5. Students' answers will vary, but may include one of the following: El pajarito **sabe** que su mamá no es un gatito, una gallina, un perro, una vaca, un automóvil, un avión o la máquina. El pajarito **sabe** que su mamá es un pájaro. El pajarito **sabe** quién es su mamá.

Guided Close Reading—Section 4 (page 52)
1. El pajarito quiere irse a su casa. El pajarito quiere estar con su mamá.
2. "¡Ay, ay, ay!", "¡Auxilio!" y "¡Bájenme de aquí!" muestran que el pajarito tiene miedo.
3. La máquina se detiene.

Making Connections—Section 4 (page 53)
The baby bird's home should be a nest in a tree. Students should have drawn a picture of their own homes.

Language Learning—Section 4 (page 55)
The words in alphabetical order are:
- avión
- barco
- gallina
- gatito
- perro
- vaca

Story Elements—Section 4 (page 56)
Students' illustrations of the settings will vary, but should correspond to the object from the story.

Story Elements—Section 4 (page 57)
- El pajarito sube muy alto en la máquina.
- Dice el pajarito: "¡Quiero estar con mi mamá!".
- La máquina devuelve el pajarito al nido.
- La mamá pájara regresa.

Comprehension Assessment (pages 65–66)
1. C. El pajarito tendrá hambre.
2. D. El pajarito no conoce el aspecto de su mamá.
3. B. Él sigue corriendo.
4. El pajarito sabe que tiene mamá y quiere encontrarla.
5. C. La máquina devuelve el pajarito al nido.

www.ingramcontent.com/pod-product-compliance
Lightning Source LLC
Chambersburg PA
CBHW060427010526
44118CB00017B/2391